STAFFORDSHIRI

by

ANTHONY POULTON-SMITH

COUNTRYSIDE BOOKS

NEWBURY · BERKSHIRE

First published 1998
© Anthony Poulton-Smith 1998

All rights reserved. No reproduction
permitted without the prior permission
of the publisher:

COUNTRYSIDE BOOKS
3 Catherine Road
Newbury, Berkshire

ISBN 1 85306 532 3

Produced through MRM Associates Ltd., Reading
Typeset by Techniset Typesetters, Merseyside
Printed by Woolnough Bookbinding Ltd., Irthlingborough

CONTENTS

The author investigating the privy at Holy Austin Rock, Kinver. This natural fold of sandstone was carved out in the middle of the 19th century.

FOREWORD

When Nicholas Battle of Countryside Books first suggested I add to the series on privies, my initial reaction was, well, unprintable. However, after a few tentative enquiries I found many people falling over themselves to relate their memories and experiences without the slightest hint of embarrassment.

The Staffordshire referred to in the title covers the county prior to the advent of the West Midlands. Thus areas to the south, such as Wolverhampton and Walsall, are included. My travels took me to stately homes, cottages, railway stations, museums, industrial sites and fields. Whilst those I met were so very different, it struck me that on this subject there can never be any class distinction. As one lady pointed out: 'All on us 'as them marks on us knees, from resting us elbows on 'em.'

It came as quite a surprise to find anyone within the county who still has an earth closet in use and even more so to find as many as I did. Unfortunately nearly all those who still used their one-holer declined my requests for photographs, but were always happy to relate their reminiscences. On one occasion I spent almost an hour convincing one elderly lady ('I'm ninety-four you know') she need not be in residence when the photograph was taken, only for her to change her mind at the last moment and not allow any pictures.

At the end of the 19th century the earth closet was as prevalent as the flush toilet is one hundred years later. Ecologically the earlier version was preferable, especially considering the concerns of water conservation today.

Hopefully these memories will stand as a reminder of an important aspect of daily life, certainly for the first half of the 20th century. Alas, this necessity of life is now a part of history and should be recorded before all traces are confined to museum pieces.

ANTHONY POULTON-SMITH

My daughter Sarah, assistant Privy researcher, posing by one of the many finds we came across on our travels through the county.

[1]

EARLY PRIVIES

In the late 20th century we take for granted the efficient disposal of sewage. The sole discomfort in the modern era is on cold winter's days when greeted with the initial shock of a cold toilet seat. Yet it was only in the Twenties that the flush toilet became standard in newly erected properties, and even then the vast majority were outside.

Except for the limited influence on sanitary conditions from the Roman occupation, little change in everyday waste disposal had taken place in Britain since man first walked these green and pleasant lands. Indeed, as the population of our islands increased and rural communities expanded into closely packed towns, the problem of sanitation grew proportionately. Buckets and pots were emptied straight from windows into the street below and if passers by were unfortunate enough to be in the line of fire, so be it.

The Biblical reference to this basic requirement instructs us to go into the desert with a paddle (wooden spade) and make a hole in the sand, the paddle also being utilised to fill in the hole afterwards. No reference to toilet paper here, nor to any alternative. The Bible also relates how Baal's temple was destroyed by the forces of Jehu (Kings II, 10:27), henceforth the place was used as a latrine. King Eglon's murder is also covered (Judges, 3:24), occurring whilst the gentleman was relieving himself in the inner room of the house.

Even the most magnificent of castles from the Middle Ages had no conveniences to speak of. Most were limited to narrow passages situated within tower walls, with the excrement dropping down a shaft to form a pile at the base – or sometimes to fall

A 1738 Hogarth illustration showing the hazard of walking beneath an open window when the chamberpots were being emptied!

The south wall of Tamworth Castle.

straight into the surrounding moat. In some of the better planned keeps one may have been lucky enough to find such places located near chimneys, which did something to keep out the cold. However, personal comfort was not at the forefront of the architect's mind, rather that the natural updraught from the fires acted as a means to remove unwanted smells.

In 1367 the first Earl of Stafford began the building of Stafford Castle. A master mason, John of Bicester, was charged with: 'Building a castle on the mound within the manor of Stafford, in length, breadth and height, with towers, rooms, bedchambers, chapel, privies, chimneys, loopholes, windows, doors and gates.' This is the earliest reference to a privy I have found within the county. It is interesting that the agreement lists privies before windows, doors and chimneys.

Monarchs both here and abroad were given little consideration when it came to a call of nature. They were more often than not under constant threat from perfidious murderers and traitors, and in order to minimise the risk of assassination the reigning sovereign would be accompanied everywhere, even to the loo. This almost proved the undoing of Frederick Barbarossa. The 12th-century German emperor found his way to one loo accompanied by so many that the wooden floor gave way under the weight. Fortunately Barbarossa managed to save himself, but several of his entourage failed to emerge alive from the pit below. The Saxon king Edmund Ironside was murdered in 1016. One chronicle records how he died when impaled on 'a spear in the fundament (backside) while at the withdraught (toilet) to purge nature'.

It was only in the 17th century that kings and queens started to receive special consideration of a sort, when commode style contraptions were introduced into the richest homes in the land.

For the rest of the population the only conveniences were public ones. In villages this would often have been over a natural

A commode at Chillington Hall, near Brewood. Architect Francis Smith of Warwick, 1724. (Photo courtesy of Staffordshire Arts and Museum Service)

watercourse of some description, whilst townsfolk would have been treated to the communal cesspit. The rural version provided its own disposal system; the cesspit needed to be emptied. However, owing to the appalling smell emanating from these places such a task would have been carried out only when the pit was overflowing. In Stafford town centre one cesspit from the 17th century was discovered during building work. It now forms part of the foundations of the Marks & Spencer's store.

A map of Stafford dating from 1625 shows how the channel in the middle of the road, principally to allow surface water to drain away, ran towards the river Sowe through the town wall at Southgate opposite the bridge. Here it discharged into the river, taking with it all the rubbish collected on the way. This would have certainly included bodily waste products (animal as well as human).

Cesspit now buried beneath Marks and Spencer in Stafford. The construction dates from the 17th century.

Gentlemen of the night. (BBC Hulton Picture Library, from *The Complete Loo* by Roger Kilroy, Victor Gollancz, 1984)

The run-off polluted the river to such a degree that the men of Stafford were obliged to cross the bridge to water their horses. Indeed this daily ritual is actually marked on the map.

To compound the problem still further, the town dung heap was located immediately downstream of this place, where the contents of the cesspits were deposited. The 1625 map identifies the dung heap and also tells us that this was the 'way to Thieves Ditch'. As this is the only reference to such a name we do not know if this was a place where thieves would hide out, or if they were deposited there as punishment. Either way it is enough to seriously make one think of going straight.

The cesspits were emptied by gongfermors. When the bucket privy arrived the same job was performed by those known as

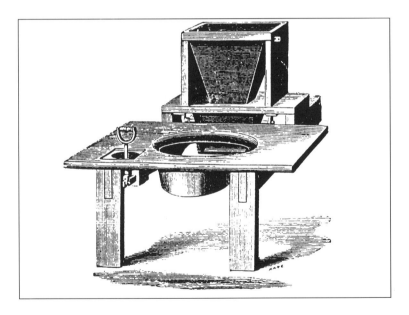

Reverend Moule's 'pull-up' earth closet of 1860.

14

night-soil men, who clearly worked at night, fundamentally to reduce the smell nuisance and the vast number of flies.

Finally, mention must be made of the automatic earth closet designed by John Parker, a cabinet-maker by trade, which improved on a manual lever-operated version invented by the Reverend Samuel Moule in 1860. In John Parker's design a series of levers were connected from the seat to a hopper. As the user rose the system released an amount of soil (or ashes) from the hopper into the bucket. Of the 20,000 made two versions were produced, in pine for the poor and mahogany for the more affluent customer.

The earth closet was soon to be pushed aside with the appearance of the flush toilet. Although in many respects it was (and is) superior to the water variety.

A commode, awaiting restoration and part of an Aladdin's cave of memorabilia collected by a lady near Eccleshall.

Regrettably, from an ecological viewpoint, the water flush did not need to be emptied and therefore it gradually reigned supreme. Should the earth closet have taken up residence in all our homes instead, today there would be few worries regarding water shortages; sewage treatment plants would have far less volume to manage and would therefore be able to work more efficiently; with fewer pipes to lag burst pipes during a thaw would be less of a hazard; and lastly we could all be producing our own garden produce – organically grown of course.

[2]

STAFFORDSHIRE'S VICTORIANS

By the middle of the 19th century the towns and cities of England were growing at a tremendous pace. The advent of the Industrial Revolution created new and more stable employment. Commuting to work over any distance was impractical, thus whole families moved to find work.

In every town, committees were formed to improve existing roads, sanitation, drains and water supplies, and to enforce these standards for the new roads and houses which were being built to accommodate the increases in population. Whilst the cobbled streets have disappeared, the sewers are still in use today. History records one family, the Clulows, who benefited from these improvements in the town of Leek.

In the 1850s the Clulows lived in a small house, which was one of ten built in two rows of five back-to-back. These properties were examples of 'jerry-built' homes, that is, erected in the shortest possible time using the cheapest materials. Unfortunately the bricks were porous and the wood soon warped, making the houses very damp places to live. There was no back garden between the rows, but merely a rough cobbled area containing two privies, an ashpit (equivalent to a dustbin) and a tap. In these times families were invariably larger than today and yet even if there was only an average of five per household, this still means that fifty individuals shared two privies and one cold water tap!

The Clulows single-mindedly set about improving their situation. Each week they saved four or five shillings with the Leek Building Society which opened in 1856. Eventually they were able to negotiate a fifteen-year mortgage and move to more salubrious premises. Their new home was to be newly built on land belonging to Joseph Billings and adjoining his timber yard in West Street.

In accordance with the new guide lines, Mr Billings sent details of his proposal to the Leek Improvement Commission. His plans showed a short new street which was to have drains leading to the newly installed town-drains, sloping cobbled streets with brick gutters and blue brick pavements. The plans were approved and construction began in 1859.

In 1860 the Clulows moved into their new home with all its modern conveniences. A tap and sink inside the house led to the drain outside, where the main differences were to be found. Instead of a cobbled yard, they had a garden where they could grow their own vegetables, and their own privy and ashpit well away from the house. Wooden doors at the back of these buildings allowed easy removal of the contents. Indeed privies and ashpits were emptied regularly by the new Refuse Collectors (another of the Leek Improvement Commissioners' ideas). These men were able to remove the contents in a wheelbarrow along a 'four-foot pathway' which connected all those in the street. This innovative idea gave the paths their name of 'wheelbarrow lanes'.

Incidentally, the street itself was anonymous when the Clulows first moved in. However, because of the obvious bend in the road the locals knew it as Angle Street.

Towards the end of the 19th century, Baswich consisted of two farms and a church and all were on the same side of the road. Not until 1900 were three homes built on the other side. No wonder then it was sometimes referred to as 'the village without a village'.

However one farm, Weeping Cross, was virtually a self-contained village in its own right. Built in the early 19th century, of timber with brick infill, the house boasted many wonderful additions. Heavy solid oak doors opened to reveal a bar, where china handled pumps drew beer from the cellar. A large coal-burning range in the kitchen could accommodate several pots and pans. One of the attic rooms boasted a big cheese press, whilst the supporting beams were lined with hooks for hanging hams.

This large home provided quarters for butlers and maids, a laundry, a blacksmith's shop, a scullery where huge built-in ovens enabled them to bake their own bread, another room had an enormous copper for boiling clothes, on the ground floor was a cheese room, and the whole house was built over a well concealed under the floor. Three separate staircases gave access to the upper floors and every room had its own fireplace.

Yet for some reason no thought was given to toilet facilities within the building. True, every room had a pot underneath the bed for use during the night, but for other times there were three-holers located at a discreet distance from the house. Each was a simple pit over which a box frame and building were erected. Three privies were available, presumably allocated by rank and/or gender, which were emptied by the farm workers on a more or less regular basis.

Stories have been passed down telling of how reluctant those who lived at Weeping Cross Farm were to visit the privy in the hours of darkness. Without electricity, the only illumination was by paraffin lamp and it was commonplace to find someone to accompany you. A practice which has been handed on to ladies (and sometimes men) of today, who never seem to visit the toilet alone when in company.

Although most Victorian towns and cities saw vast improvements in sanitation, there was always the exception to prove the proverbial rule. Staffordshire's exception was undoubtedly Stone.

The pot beneath the bed.

Some buckets were fitted with decorative 'basins'.
(Photo courtesy of Twyford & Doulton)

Without electricity, a paraffin lamp in the privy came in very handy.

The pleasant market town we find today owes a very great deal to the efforts of Dr Edward Fernie MD, who pressed continually for the local authorities to improve upon the appalling condition of the open sewers, cesspits and the Scotch Brook, which was more pollution than water.

In 1865 there were 25 deaths from cholera. By 1873 enteric fever was reaching epidemic proportions. Over the period from 1870 to the end of 1873, there were 104 deaths from specified diseases. Out of this number no less than 39 died as a result of diarrhoea and 25 from the fever. Added to this were the innumerable cases who were removed from the district, on the orders of practitioners, to be treated in Stafford Infirmary.

In an attempt to improve matters Dr Fernie wrote to the Guardians of the Local Government Board in London and, in January 1874 a Medical Officer, Dr Ballard, inspected the town. His report was published in June of that year and made gruesome reading. Of particular interest are his findings as to the privies in Stone. This report is so graphic it is reproduced here:

As to Privy Arrangements and Excrement Nuisances

There are very few water-closets in Stone. Both in the town and in the villages about it the cesspit-privy is in ordinary use. The cesspit usually extends from beneath the privy seat to some distance on one side or at the rear of the privy, or else it is entirely at the side or the rear. In some instances the opening to the cesspit is covered more or less closely by a stone or iron plate; but in very many cases the cesspit is entirely open or only covered partially and imperfectly by a few boards so that the excrement is entirely exposed to view. All the cesspits of the latter kind which I saw were full, and some of them overflowing. In many instances these cesspits are close to inhabited houses, and in some instances against the walls of houses.

I have rarely, if ever, seen anything more disgusting than some of these cesspit-privies. Perhaps the most disgusting of all was situated against the wall of a house in a narrow, close, unwholesome court leading out of Church Street and known as Goblin's Hole, where one dilapidated privy, scarcely approachable for filth, was provided for the use of the inhabitants of six or seven houses. The excrement beneath the seat was entirely exposed. One of the inhabitants of this court informed me that the Inspector of Nuisances had not been in the court, to her knowledge, for six months. There are several places in the town where the emptying of privy cesspits can only be effected by carrying the contents through dwelling-houses. Some dwellings (for example in Newcastle Street) have no privy accommodation at all.

In other instances, the accommodation provided is very insufficient, as, for instance, in a row of five cottages in the Old Oulton Road, where one privy, open to the road and free to all passers by, is provided for the use of thirty-five persons inhabiting the cottages. In one instance, in Church Street, the inhabitants of seven cottages have been without any privy accommodation for a period of nine weeks in consequence of the privy having been blown down by the wind. The Inspector of Nuisances knew of the street but had not caused the fault to be remedied. In the same row of cottages there were privies discharging their contents into an open ditch about three or four yards from the rear of the dwellings. The instances of excrement nuisances given above are only a few examples of the very large number which I observed in all parts of the town and its outskirts. I am informed that the people who remove the excrement often (I was told, commonly) do it in the day time to the great annoyance of the passers by. The Rural Sanitary Authority leaves it with the occupiers to make their own arrangements with these people.

Examples of early 20th-century finery on display at Caradon Bathrooms. (Photo courtesy of Twyford & Doulton)

In the main, sanitary conditions in Victorian towns were of the highest order. This report shows there were blots on the landscape but also proves that, with a little pressure, the governing bodies were more than capable of dealing with those who did not conform to the new standards laid down. It should be noted that a brass plaque in Christ Church commemorates the work of Dr Edward Fernie in ridding Stone of its problem. It bears the inscription 'erected by public subscription' – a fitting testament to the grateful thanks of the people of Stone for his pivotal role in getting the Board of Guardians to toe the legislative line on improvements in sanitation and waste disposal.

The development of the flush toilet, with all its ecological shortcomings, flourished in the county under the influence of

Certainly part of Thomas Twyford's bathroom equipment but what? Labelled 'The Mystery', not even the present company have any idea what it was. (Photo courtesy of Twyford & Doulton)

Thomas Twyford. Indeed, the name of Twyford and also Doulton, are synonymous with bathroom fittings even to this day. Both concerns lived on after the deaths of their founders and are now important brand names within the Caradon Plumbing Company.

When I visited Terry Woollescroft at Caradon, I was shown the unique collection of Twyford and Doulton Victorian loos set out in a new gallery in their foyer. These museum pieces include the celebrated 'Mystery Object', the use of which is unknown even to these experts.

[3]

'When I Was Young'

Talke-o'-th'-Hill is a very small place. However, it certainly produced a number of long-lived individuals judging by the number of memories it evoked. Mrs Eva Hancock spoke to me of her time at St Saviour's School at Cole Hill in the village. The school had two four-holers, one each for the boys and girls, which lay on opposite sides of the iron railings which also served to segregate the two playgrounds. The waste from these ran into a narrow channel which then drained off to join the local river system. The school still stands but the privies, and even the church after which it was named, are no more.

Another former resident of Talke-o'-th'-Hill, Annie Bath (née Stevenson), remembers the two-holer they had when she was a girl. It was not unusual for adults and children to be in occupation at the same time, using suitably sized holes, whilst toddlers who could not yet reach the seat were provided with a porcelain potty. The whole building was located some twenty-five yards from the house, behind a large bank of earth, which had to be negotiated in both directions. When wet or frozen this in itself was a major obstacle to relief. In later years Annie attended Talke Girls School. Here the girls used an eight or ten-holer, however each was separated into private cubicles (a luxury). Unfortunately a rota system operated where the girls had to take a turn at cleaning the privy, although (thankfully) emptying the buckets was not their responsibility.

In 1938 Mr J. Allcock, now of Bournebrook, Birmingham, moved into a house with his new bride. Not long after they had taken up residence his wife came rushing into the house screaming. 'I can't use that, it's a disgrace.' On investigation Mr Allcock discovered the source of his wife's dismay. The toilet consisted of a wooden seat on top of a pipe approximately eight feet in length, two feet above ground, the remainder below. A hatchway enabled him to discover a collection device below the pipe, which not only served the privy but also collected all the rainwater from the guttering. When the contents reached a certain level the whole was tipped into the sewers. A quick visit to the local council resulted in a return to Mrs Allcock's acquired taste – the flush toilet.

Eileen Matthews remembers her childhood privy consisting of an old coal bucket underneath a board with a rather large hole cut in it (the previous occupant must have been on the large side). She clearly recalls having to hang onto the sides in order to prevent her falling through. The seat was scrubbed and bleached every day. Their house was one of three built around 1700; the village post office and the manor house stood at the front, their home was at the back. Being off the road they were not always visited by the man with the cart, and were forced to dispose of the contents when the bucket was full. When Eileen's father died it was down to her mother and herself to manhandle the heavy bucket and its contents to a hole in the earth which they had dug. Such was the great weight they would often 'slip and slop', ending up with much of the contents upon their persons.

The job of emptying the contents had to be done by someone. This unenviable task was performed by a gentleman known in polite conversation as 'the muck-man'. In Woodstock, Stoke-on-Trent, this task was performed at one time by Joe Lovatt. His granddaughter, Margaret Hall, told me how Mrs Lovatt made her husband go to the shed when he returned from work. There he would remove his work clothing and wash using a bucket of water which his wife would provide along with clean attire. Joe was not allowed within yards of the house until he had accomplished this task to Mrs Lovatt's satisfaction.

Mr J. East of Walsall, now retired, recalls his early working life. Whilst the first part of his narrative has nothing to do with privies, it is worthy of inclusion for its happy ending. At the age of eighteen he was employed in a factory to time a certain number of young ladies for each new item they produced. One day his employer falsely accused him of adjusting the times for one girl,

Rose, which resulted in her receiving five shillings extra in her pay. Mr East promptly left that employment and, despite being begged to return, found another job at twice the pay. The increased wage was to prove of great benefit to him for he was able to afford to marry in 1942. His wife for the next forty-six years was none other than Rose.

On the second day of Mr East's new employ, at Rubery-Owen of Darlaston, he asked the location of the toilet and was pointed in the direction of one available to him. On entering the building he was amazed, not to say embarrassed, to find ten men occupying half of the twenty holes cut into a board above a pit. Unlike his earlier employment, there were no dividing screens to offer any privacy and, to make matters worse, someone was entrusted with the task of supplying each visitor with paper and ensuring that none stayed away from their work for too long! Alas I was unable to discover how the attendant managed to time all his visitors. Furthermore, I am intrigued as to what was considered 'adequate' time for a visit and indeed just how much this fellow was paid for wielding such awesome power.

In 1923 Mr Larner, then just five years old, went to live with foster parents in Burton-on-Trent. The family home in Queen Street was fronted by a fish and chip shop. Mr Larner has clear memories of the privy, for it was not something he had encountered in his short life: 'The other side of Queen Street all had flush toilets, but our lot had to wait 'til Thursday night 'cos that were when the night-soil men came. First came a cart, a bit like the old dray, drawn by two horses. It carried all the clean pans that went under the board in the privy. Each pan was about three feet across, and about two-and-a-half feet deep. There were two handles so the men could carry 'em. Must have been heavy when they were full, for it took two on 'em to carry the full 'un.

Night-soil men at work around 1900, thought to be in Walsall. (Photo courtesy of Staffordshire Arts and Museum Service)

'The night-soil men got round to the back by the entry which ran between the houses, us 'n next door. There they'd take out the full pan and drop the clean 'un in its place. This they'd carry out to the street where it were emptied into a tanker on a second cart, which were also horse-drawn. The used pans were put on the first cart and the men would move further up the street. I heard it said that the pans were cleaned with tar gas, which not only cleaned 'em but acted as a disinfectant.

'Luckily the next year, almost on my sixth birthday, they put in a flush toilet. It took the place of the old coal hole at the back of the house and the old privy became the new coal hole. When they fitted the waste pipe from the toilet to the sewers, they had to lift all the bricks from the floor in the entry.

'In 1993 I went back to see if the place were still there. Number ninety-four still stood, although it weren't a chip shop no more. I walked up the entry and had a look round the back and quite a few of the old privies were still standing. Of course today they're used as sheds. When I walked round I had to watch me step, 'cos the cobbles up the entry were all over the place, from when they took 'em up to put in the drainage.'

One long-time resident of a village just outside Eccleshall remembers a great deal of her experiences. As a young girl in Eccleshall she recalls all the pans were made by a local black-smith. A man was employed by a character known as 'Dodger' Lindup (she never found out how he earned this nickname) to empty the pans and take the contents on a horse-drawn metal-lined cart to the sewage works. As with many places the pans had to be carried through the houses as there was no access to the rear of the property from the street. In order to minimise the inconvenience (not to mention the smell) he called around three or four o'clock in the morning.

The privy itself was always kept scrupulously clean. After the weekly wash had been hung out to dry, and the water in the copper had cooled a little, they used the soapy water in which their clothes had been washed to scrub the inside of the privy.

When she married she moved into a cottage in one of the small villages just outside Eccleshall. Here the pan was replaced by a bucket. This was made for the purpose and had a lip on either side to prevent the contents from spilling when the bucket was emptied. In her new home she did not have the luxury of having someone call round to empty the privy. Instead all the villagers dug a deep hole in the garden and, when necessary, emptied the bucket into it. The hole was big enough to last for a whole year, at the end of which the contents were dug into the vegetable garden and a new hole made.

An outside flush toilet was installed in 1951. However, an

32

Original privy bucket recently used to grow a selection of flowers. Note the side handle and shaped lip to aid emptying without spillage.

electric light was not fitted until several years later which meant many a long walk down the garden with lantern held high on long winter nights.

Although the privy is now unrecognisable (being used to store the coal) the bucket is still put to good use, flowers being grown in it year after year.

The mill house at Audley was once home to the uncle and aunt of Jan Francis. She vividly remembers the many happy times she stayed with her relatives at the mill as a young girl. In particular she recalls the privy, which was built over the run-off from the mill after the water had turned the mill wheel and ran on to rejoin the stream known as Shraley Brook.

As there had always been a large number of people (of varying ages) living in the house, the privy was designed to accommodate all-comers (whether individually or in groups). Jan told me that her aunt kept it scrupulously clean, scrubbing the pine seat regularly. Mrs Francis thought (or perhaps hoped) the building might have survived, however when I visited the mill all traces had vanished. This was a great disappointment as it would have made a wonderful illustration, not only for its unique position over the brook, but for the seat with seven holes inside. This was by far the largest seater in a private residence I discovered when preparing this book.

This former privy at Stanton is now a tool shed. However, the hole in the side for emptying is still apparent.

Listening to memories of privy emptying and disposal made me realise that it was only in the larger places that this job provided permanent employment. In smaller village areas – when they had the luxury of an emptying service – it was often performed by anyone who had the right equipment necessary for transporting the waste.

One gentleman told me of a local firm of builders, who used an early flat-bed truck. For most of the week this transported construction materials and equipment. However, on Thursdays the builders (and their truck) trundled around the local lanes emptying the ashpits (which were often found next to privies) resulting from the many coal fires. That evening the truck would travel the circuit a second time. The truck, by now well-laden with the ashes collected that day, would be used to transport the contents of the privies. As the buckets were emptied the ashes would soak up much of the waste, making disposal of both items together much easier than either of them individually.

By Friday morning the builders were back to their main trade in the construction industry – and looking forward to their slightly larger pay packets as a result of the extra hours put in the previous day as night-soil men.

[4]

THE WAR YEARS

It has always intrigued me just how many memories of the war years are of a humorous nature. Of course in such troubled times the lighter moments provide a welcome respite from the hardship of everyday life and worries of absent loved ones. Thus it came as no surprise to find a sizable number of privy memories dating from the Second World War. Indeed there were sufficient to devote a whole chapter to these six years.

David Evans recalled being stationed at Portsmouth with the Royal Navy. The dockers were seen to descend upon the privy at break times, which interested the young military men greatly. A small watercourse ran underneath this eight-holer, providing a natural sewerage system for disposal straight into the sea. Before long the sailors had devised a way of putting their naval training to good use.

They would build a small raft on which they placed paper, rags, indeed anything which would burn readily. This would then be lovingly set aflame and with full military honours launched upon the small stream. As it floated under the dockers' privy the navy men took great delight in hearing the shouts and screams from the dockers as the flames reached the uncovered flesh of those seated within. The dockers soon grew wary of the navy's pranksters and the scramble at the beginning of the break was as much for the hole farthest downstream as for the relief sought therein.

This practical joke was related to me time and again (notably from ex-miners). One comes from Mr Arthur Brown of Stoke-on-Trent, who described his memories so eloquently it could never do the tale justice unless related in his own words:

'In 1931 I joined the army, and at my hutted barracks in Blackdown near Aldershot I once more came across the out-buildings containing "buckets latrine, soldiers for the use of", proving that the War Office had not yet modernised itself in even this basic necessity. The fact that the Germans were well ahead and waiting to pounce meant nothing.

'These "buckets latrine", being army issue, were made to fit the underside of the cubicle and as they were withdrawn for emptying by a small door at the rear it meant that if an unfortu-nate soldier was sitting above, innocent of the work going on beneath him, the scraping as the bucket latrine was dragged away often brought a howl of agony from the victim. If it hap-pened to be a sergeant there would be celebrations in the Naafi that evening.

'When travelling abroad to a posting in those days there was only one way, a troopship. To me a cruise ship. Oh! What a boring time the modern soldiers must have in a transport plane. We cruised ten days or more in a ship to Egypt. Hundreds of sol-diers on the *Neuralia*, for example. How was the privy problem overcome? Leave it to the army.

'On each troop deck, to serve several hundred soldiers there existed a row of open-fronted seats, numbering about thirty, above a long trough containing sea water pumped up at one end and running beneath the over-fed squaddies to be ejected back into the sea, carrying its burden as a gift to the fish. All were contented that a continuous supply of fresh water was catering to their needs. No smell, food for the fish, plenty of Army Form Blank, happiness all round. Very good, you will remark. Nice and hygienic. But what an opportunity for the old sweat who has seen it all before. There was always one to upset the apple cart.

' "Watch this," said a Geordie of the Durham Light Infantry. Interested as I was, having not quite two years service behind me, I watched as he pretended to use the upper end seat as soon as it became vacant. Carefully hiding his action he took from his pocket a postcard-size piece of thick cardboard on which he stuck a small stub of candle. Lighting this he floated it in the slowly moving stream of water. Like a child with a firework he retired immediately, as did I, mingling with the crowd toing and froing.

'His Geordie visage took on a glow of happiness as he listened to the Oh's, Ow's, Groo's, Geroff's and yells of agony as the candle floated on its merry way to the sea. On my future daily visits to this establishment I always made sure I occupied the upper end seat.'

A gentleman by the name of Bill Elliott once lived just north of Lichfield at Fradley. The nearby aerodrome, still visible to the west from the A38, provided a base for Lancaster bombers in the Forties. Each night that these huge planes limped back from their night-time bombing raids in the early hours Mr Elliott noted they passed progressively lower above his roof. 'They'll take bloody roof off one night, gal,' he told his wife next morning.

After several weeks of this, there came the night that Mr Elliott was woken by the noise of the spluttering, straining engines of a bomber nearing their home. Waking his wife, he virtually threw her down the stairs where they both took shelter under the kitchen table as the house shook from the approaching Lancaster. To their disbelief the noise of the aeroplane diminished and their home remained intact and the couple returned to bed.

On waking the next morning Mrs Elliott was led to the window by her husband, 'Just take a look outside.' As she peered into the morning gloom she noticed the rear fence was broken. Then she saw how it had happened. The privy, or what remained of it, had been ripped from the garden, through the fence, and lay some yards into the field beyond. Their house had escaped, barely, but the bomber flew so low the under-carriage had demolished the privy.

Recollections from Eccleshall Historical Society include those from the Civil Defence covering Chebsey, Norton Bridge, Shal-lowford, Hilcote and Slindon. Such a large area took a number of men to cover it and soldiers were often called in from Liver-pool to relieve the sparse local volunteers.

Edwin Silvester worked for Mr Downes on his farm at Cheb-sey and was on night duty there when one young man was cele-brating his birthday. As was customary, his companions put him in a blanket and tossed him in the air, once for each year of his life. Such humour was not appreciated by the birthday boy. He took off in a terrible rage and his whereabouts was a mystery until he was heard venting his anger by emptying his rifle on the privy on the other side of the field, much to the consternation of a Mr Bickley, who was in residence at the time!

Main line sewage did not arrive at Eccleshall until after the war, and until then the night-soil men continued to empty the privies. In an effort to keep the smell problem to a minimum they collected late at night. Many tenement blocks had no access to the rear, which meant they were forced to walk through the house with the bucket and its contents.

Steve Bradbury recalls his mother telling him she looked after the night-soil men, 'It reminds them not to spill anything when they walk through the house.' She used to give them bread and cheese or a cup of tea, but none of them ever bothered to wash before they ate or drank.

Unlike many war memories, rationing stories usually lack any humorous tone. However, Jessy Smith recalls one of her neighbours commenting on how wonderful it was to eat tomatoes again and thanked her for pointing her in the direction of someone who grew his own and sold them to neighbours at a very reasonable price.

'Lord knows how he manages to grow them so big and tasty,' she said to Jessy.

'Don't you know?' replied Jessy. 'Because he won't have the night-soil men walking through his house with the contents of the privy, he empties it over his vegetable patch.'

Jessy watched as the colour drained from her friend's face. Never again did she purchase vegetables from this source, despite the shortage of fresh vegetables which continued for several years.

Whilst most towns and cities were treated to the luxury of flush toilets, the villages often had to wait until after the war.

Colton, like many others, took its share of evacuees. The local children here saw their new friends from the big city as heroes, having braved the bombing raids in shelters. When Colton witnessed the occasional bomb near the railway line, or once an incendiary device falling on the marshes, it became the focal point of interest for weeks.

Many of the children came from Birmingham. They were horrified by the blackness of the country night, and could never comprehend how anyone could survive with just one shop, no cinema, no chip shop, and only three buses each week. Village sanitation appalled the evacuees. Buckets or pits at the end of the garden caused problems. They refused to go out into the night with a candle or lamp. Consequently there were wet beds.

The local children felt really sorry for their friends from the city, they hated the dark too. Rats and mice often ran over feet whilst they sat. Cows would rub and stamp at the rear of the privy. Paper, when it was available, was always damp. One recalled when they had run out of paper: 'We used to holler for help at the back door, as it was left open a crack, until Mum came with two or three sheets of paper.'

[5]

OTHER THINGS WENT DOWN
THE PRIVY

One of my first thoughts when considering this book was the subject of toilet paper. Many will recall the use of newspaper before the soft, quilted, super-absorbent tissue of the modern era. But newspaper, too, must have been a fairly recent accessory. A review of the items utilised by our ancestors is a positive education.

Aside from the Roman era, when natural sponges were used to wash the area in question, until medieval times grass, leaves, bark, even stones were all that was available. By the 15th century we know the rich used old clothing cut into squares specifically for the purpose. The poor, however, continued to use anything to hand.

Little change until the Victorian years saw the appearance of 'Gayety's Medicated Paper' in 1857, which was sold in flat packs and only available from chemists. To avoid embarrassment on the part of the customer the product was not put on display but discreetly handed over on request. Bromo Water Closet's paper boasted 'The Highest Prize Awarded at the Paris Exposition of 1878'. 'Novio Pure Manila Toilet Packet' arrived in 1928. It was described as 'antiseptic, thin, soft, strong & silky', and was the first to be sold on a roll. Soft tissue-style paper appeared four years later but proved less popular at first. The next time you shop for colour coordinated toilet tissue for your bathroom, you should recall that coloured paper did not appear until 1957.

The *Daily Mail* was always popular.

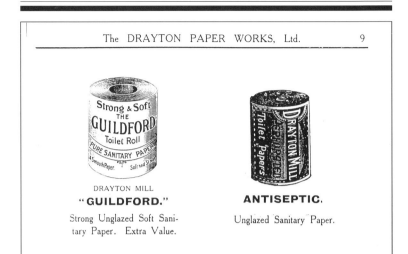

DRAYTON MILL
"GUILDFORD."

Strong Unglazed Soft Sanitary Paper. Extra Value.

ANTISEPTIC.

Unglazed Sanitary Paper.

Companies like the Drayton Paper Works not only began to supply toilet rolls but also the holders on which to hang them.

"Drayton Mill" Toilet Roll Holders.

"No. 1,"
4/= doz. net.
STOCKED IN
Nickelled, Brassed and Bronzed.

Holders Mounted on Backboards.

			Per doz. net.
No. 1	...	...	**11/-**
Crown	...	...	**13/6**

On Mirrors. Per doz. net.

No. 1	...	...	**25/-**
Crown	...	...	**27/6**

Backboards or Mirrors. Per doz. net.

Solid Mahogany (French Polished)			**7/-**
Oak	...	...	**7/-**
Mirrors (Bevelled)	...	...	**21/-**

"The Crown,"
6/6 doz. net.
STOCKED IN
Nickelled, Brassed and Bronzed.

Aside from that which the privy was designed to take, a number of the tales I heard on my travels covered other objects which would have fared better had they not ventured into the void which lay beneath the wooden seat. Hats, spectacles, false teeth and coinage seemed particularly susceptible, although I also heard of two watches, an earring, a necklace and a tobacco pipe. Yet the only items which were remembered as retrieved were the hats and the teeth!

Mrs Nora Hand lived with her mother and father at the home of her grandparents in Gordon Street, Burslem. At the end of the Forties, when she was seven, she recalls the ducket in the back yard. A ducket was a revolving mill wheel affair, which tipped the contents into the local sewerage system as the weight turned the wheel. To Nora and her brother, who is a year younger, the pit underneath the seat appeared vast and they constantly worried about falling in.

One day while they were playing in the garden they heard a terrible commotion emanating from the privy and went to investigate. They discovered a cat which had somehow managed to fall through the hole and was trapped within the pit. For what seemed like the whole day they tried to free the poor animal using hooks, ropes, or sticks. The rescue equipment always ended up in the same place as the cat. After they returned to try again with yet another stick they found the cat had disappeared. They presumed it had fallen through to the drainage system below. Never did they discover to whom the cat belonged, or even hear of anyone who had lost their pet.

Norah has another marvellous story, this one involving the luxurious flush toilet that three years later replaced the old ducket. Her grandmother, one Eliza Cope, was feared by all who knew her. Barely five feet tall, Eliza was, in Nora's words, 'a right old battleaxe'. However, when the toilet was installed it was grandmother's pride and joy.

45

About one week after the toilet's arrival, Nora and her brother were playing football with a rather large and heavy stone, when a kick from one of them directed the stone through the open toilet door. When they went to retrieve it they discovered a huge crack in the toilet pan, evidently made by the impact of their stone 'football'. Mum, dad and even grandpa could not bring themselves to break the news to the old woman and so a plan was drawn up.

They collected together all the cash they could raise in order to purchase a replacement toilet. Here lay a big problem. Two different toilets were sold. The original outside version was a cream colour and thicker and taller than the interior white toilet. However, they had only sufficient money to purchase the cheaper indoor model. At length they decided to go ahead and buy the pure white one. Arrangements were made to replace the damaged toilet whilst Eliza was out. The switch was made successfully, and despite living for a further thirty years in the same house, the 'battleaxe' never noticed the change.

A gentleman in Tean remembers having their first 'proper' toilet. Whilst it was connected to the sewerage system, it had no flush. Therefore it was the family's practice to empty the contents of the washing-up bowl down the toilet thrice daily, irrespective of use.

[6]

PUBLIC PRIVIES

Today public conveniences are, in the main, easy to locate and scrupulously clean. All establishments selling refreshments are required by law to provide facilities for patrons to relieve themselves. Clearly this was not always the case. Rows of houses often shared communal privies and when sewers and road surfaces were only just beginning to be thought about, public lavatories were well down on the list of priorities.

In present-day towns public toilets are found at several street locations, similarly at every sizable store. Before the advent of the flush toilet or the privy people went in the most convenient and private place they could. When several members of the same household shared a one-holer, busy times of the day often led to a queue. In towns neighbours would make use of each other's privy in order to resolve the problem. However, in rural areas the distances between conveniences made this impractical.

As the needs of those in the queue became increasingly urgent, they would return to the habits of their ancestors and go for 'a country one'. For the most part paper was a luxury confined to the privy and, unless one had the foresight to take a supply with you, any serviceable vegetation was sought out. Dock leaves were a particular favourite, although anything from handfuls of grass or leaves to a suitably shaped snowball were utilised.

The 'country one' must have had its problems during the colder months. Unfortunately many trees have an annoying habit of defoliating in the autumn leading to three problems: less natural cover is given from bare branches; dried leaves do not provide the same service as the fresh green variety; and not least 'the chill factor'!

This brick-built farm privy pictured near Yoxall was once a very 'public convenience'.

otice the buckets still in situ. (Photos courtesy of Staffordshire Arts and Museum Service)

At home these problems were easily overcome. But people had to travel. For those in the many villages dotted around the county a weekly trip to the nearest town provided their only opportunity to purchase items not available locally.

Towards the end of the 19th century the day outing became increasingly popular, too. Such trips often involved two or three hours travel on a long horse-drawn float on which wooden benches were laid. The solution to the toilet problem came in the shape of an elongated potty. This was no embarrassment for young children; the ladies' privacy was ensured by their long dresses of the period; whilst the men caught up with the float again after disappearing behind a hedge. The contents, of course, were disposed of simply by emptying the potty over the side as they moved along.

I am indebted to Bob Meason who pointed me in the direction of a 'public privy' little more than a stone's throw from my home. Any discomfiture at my ignorance was somewhat tempered when I discovered that some of those who worked at the building that contains it were completely unaware of its existence.

Clifton Campville boasts a splendid church in comparison with the size of the village. St Andrew's has, in fact, been described as the finest medieval parish church in Staffordshire, and is mentioned in Domesday. The spire, supported by flying buttresses, is visible for many miles.

The two-storeyed north transept is the earliest surviving part of the building, on the upper floor being situated a priest's retreat. Recently refurbished, this dates from the Early English period (circa 1300). Climbing the narrow, twisting stone staircase I emerged into a room measuring approximately four metres by three metres. Directly opposite the door I found the garderobe, the old name given to privies built into the thickness of a stone wall in a large house, castle – or church. Unlike other garderobes I located, this one is positioned in the corner and not along the straight wall.

Although no board remains the ingenious workings of this system are better appreciated from outside. Much of the rain falling on this side of the church is channelled into what appears to be at first glance a chimney pot underneath the guttering. However, it does in fact serve the same function as the modern cistern, although there is no storage of the rainwater for an on-demand flush. The water is directed down into the base of the garderobe and washes away the contents. These do not drop down outside the walls as with most toilets of the type, but are allowed to drain through a stone which has had several holes bored into it.

The resulting liquid is then sent down the outside of the wall to the drain dug around the whole of the church. I fully appreciated how the architecture of the building cleverly directs the dirty water to the drain. Indeed, so beautifully was this accomplished in the 14th-century original that modern additions of plastic guttering and modern drains follow the identical pathways and locations.

As a footnote to this find, the ladies who were cleaning the church were very interested in examining this priest's retreat, paying particular attention to the garderobe. Recently some of the parishioners have suggested a public toilet should be incorporated within the church. A suggestion which has appalled others as 'a church is no place for a toilet'. These ladies would welcome such an addition for their own comfort and were looking forward to informing those who disapproved that a toilet had been in place at St Andrew's for over five hundred years!

The garderobe in the priest's retreat at St Andrew's, Clifton Campville. The natural

flush provided by rainwater can be clearly seen from the outside.

A former three-holer behind the church at Mucklestone.

Whilst not a privy, mention must be made of the underground Victorian toilet at the North Stafford Hotel in Stoke. This wondrous piece of art nouveau is a gents' toilet and was brought to my attention by Barbara Adams of BBC Radio Stoke.

On entering the toilet one descends a marvellous green and white tiled staircase, with an ornate brass handrail complementing the tiling superbly. The first thing that catches the eye are four tiles beautifully lettered LA-VA-TO-RY, the surround of each letter being hand formed with a glaze infill. The tiles date from around 1890, slightly later than the hotel itself. The handrail reaches the bottom, leading one towards walls and floors of varying shades of green, peach and cream, with a ceiling of stylised blue tulips. The subtlety of the colour scheme is unlike the modern clinical colours we now use, and lends to the overall effect. All of the corners are rounded, the tiles having been pressed in a specially designed mould using dust clay.

What I found truly remarkable was the pristine condition of the tiles which, despite being over one hundred years old, have never needed replacing. Horizontal lines link vertical panels where friezes of contemporary scenes are depicted. The lines serve to draw the eye from one picture to the next.

Toilets of similar age are rare. To have retained the original design to this degree may well be unique. However, the site still has an even bigger surprise up its sleeve.

Originally the toilet formed the hotel end of a tunnel which led from Stoke station. Travellers would leave their train at platform 1 and descend the staircase. Here the tunnel led them underneath the road to the North Stafford Hotel, via the toilet. (Needless to say this route was for men only.)

However, the pièce de résistance is revealed when the door to the tunnel is unlocked, for here there is the original ticket collector's office. The oak bench and panels are still in place, as are almost one hundred brass coat hooks.

Underground toilet at Stoke-on-Trent, its Victorian splendour remarked upon as 'wasted on the men'. See photos on pages 57 and 58

Today the tunnel is sealed off just past the ticket collector's booth at a point roughly corresponding with the road above. Indeed, we are no longer certain as to the direction of the tunnel, other than the clues offered by the floor tiling. Perhaps one day the tunnel will be reopened as a museum but, until then, what remains of the underground Victorian toilet stands as a reminder of 19th-century craftsmanship.

[7]

OTHER PRIVIES

It came as some surprise to find the number of properties, in particular around the Staffordshire Moorlands, which still have a privy as their only form of sanitation. What is more they still have the 1990s' version of the 1890s' night-soil man calling on them to empty the bucket every week.

I have to report that the majority of privy owners were reluctant to allow me to photograph their property, or even to talk about it. However, Dennis Bailey of Woodwall Green was one who proudly gave me a guided tour of his hand-built privy. The cart, today powered by a diesel engine, arrives each week to empty the contents and deposit a clean bucket under the seat.

Not far from here, at Fairoak, lives Mrs Turtle. Undoubtedly her old brick privy was the most sturdy construction I saw on my travels. Not for several years has the building been used, indeed when I saw it the interior was still fitted out for their hens, with access provided (for the hens) by the same hole through which the privy had once been emptied. Not only the bucket and seat had disappeared, but so also had the hens, although the roosts were still there.

The farm had previously belonged to Mrs Turtle's father. When the new flush toilet had been installed it was suggested that the privy be demolished, but her father would not hear of it. Even since his death Mrs Turtle has resisted any idea of demolishing the building, for it was something her father was very attached to as, unlike the new indoor toilet, here there was never a queue.

The Shugborough Estate, east of Stafford, provided me with three privy examples. The first is situated at the rear of the farm

59

New top, old bottom! The plastic seat lifts off in order to empty the bucket, which still happens every Tuesday.

Dennis Bailey's privy, still in use. The lid, while still present, is 'never used'.

Mrs Turtle's former privy was one of the sturdiest buildings I found.

The rear view shows where the hens gained access through the emptying hole.

This privy on the Shugborough Estate was in use until the farm closed in
1974. Now the only likely occupants are geese.

building in an area now occupied by geese (who noisily objected
to our invasion of their space). This privy is thought to have been
erected at the same time as the rest of the buildings, in 1805. I
was informed that it was in use right up to the time when the
last occupants left in 1975. It seems for the last twenty years the
privy, now minus its door, has been used as a store for excess
timber, for several loads had to be removed in order to gain
access.

A second example has been erected in the museum itself.
However, this is no artificial construction but was removed
from a farm at Yoxall some years ago and transferred to the
museum. The staff here have done a marvellous job of restoring
it to its former glory, and housing it in a suitable display.
Authentic in every detail, there is even a nail in the wall from

The seat, bucket and door of this outdoor privy from a farm at Morrey, near Yoxall, were rescued in 1994 and relocated in the Staffordshire County Museum at Shugborough. (Photo courtesy of Staffordshire Arts and Museum Service)

Two-holer, with one lid intact, now displayed between the present-day ladies and gents toilets at the children's farm at Shugborough.

which hangs a length of string tying together a wad of torn newspaper.

Shugborough's last contribution is in the form of a two-holer, one open and the other having its lid intact, although only the board survives. Amusingly, someone had had the idea of hanging it from the wall between the modern ladies and gents in the farm display.

Eddie Craik remembers moving to Hixon as a boy in 1936. All the houses in the area still had privies, only the more affluent members of the community could afford the luxury of a flush toilet.

Eddie recalls marvelling at something he had never seen

before – a three-holer at the public baths in Hixon. Such a con-struction would certainly have proven useful at home, particu-larly when his mother and sisters used to 'go' together as none of them would make the journey down the garden on dark nights. A walk of some fifty yards. All the houses had to negotiate this long walk to their privy. On cold nights such a jaunt was particularly daunting and most of the men simply went 'round the corner' to 'hang out'. Indeed if the weather was particularly inclement it was not unheard of to go on the newspaper in front of the fire. The sitter then made the result into a parcel which was dropped outside the back door until morning.

Their particular privy, a one-holer, had a small step added to give easier access for the children for the seat was otherwise too high. There was no bucket underneath, but a simple pit measur-ing 5 feet by 6 feet. This was emptied in the spring of each year, and it was always Eddie's job. First a long trench was dug along-side the path to the privy. Not an easy undertaking as this was fifty yards in length. Next he called at a local farm to borrow the 'muck barrow' and made numerous trips from privy to trench moving all that had accumulated over the year.

When this leg of the task was over and the trench had been refilled, it was left to lie for four to six weeks. With the natural fertiliser and recent tilling of the soil, this area was quickly uti-lised to grow vegetables. The Craiks always planted kidney beans, for they produced a bumper crop which enabled them to swap the excess for other vegetables grown by neighbours. 'They grew everything,' recalls Eddie, 'everything but root crops, potatoes and such. Well, if they did try carrots, or parsnips, it were just the once. You could taste it you see, the muck like. When I served in Korea during the Fifties, we made sure all our vegetables were imported, 'cos the locals used the same field for growing vegetables as they did for their toilet.'

Mr Craik also told me of one local character, who was noted

Traditional emptying scoop – no wonder the operation took so long!

for his unsociable behaviour. So strong was this elderly gentle-man's desire for privacy that he dug himself a private toilet in the field under a hawthorn. However, should he be spotted by any of the local children on his way to his private privy, his soli-tude would often be invaded. Taunts, rustling bushes and a chorus of suitable accompanying sounds were sure to rouse the man's short temper.

Prior to researching this book I was blissfully unaware of some of the more unusual sites which I was later fortunate enough to visit. Without a doubt one of the most delightful is the privy at the Holy Austin Rock at Kinver.

This sandstone cliff, known as Kinver Edge, looms imposingly over the surrounding countryside, its silhouette masked by the many trees which grow along and about its sides. During the Middle Ages a natural cavern was used for many years as a retreat by a monk (hence the 'Holy'). In the middle of the 19th century, however, local workers carved out twelve homes in the face of the sandstone. In truth these must have been extremely cramped, even by the standards of the time. Each residence was equipped with a man-made front, while the inner walls were the reddish-orange hue of the rock itself. Several of the frontages have been restored and are open to visitors at certain times throughout the warmer months. Those which have not been renovated show how these people actually created holes for doors and windows in the rock.

There were two communal privies for the dozen families. One, a brick-built structure, no longer stands but the other is of great interest. Standing in front and slightly lower down the slope is an uplift in the rock strata, luckily away from the well head. Here they hollowed out the arch-like shape in the sand-stone to produce an artificial cave which was used as a privy.

Some of the houses cut into the face of the sandstone at Kinver. The lower picture shows how the holes for the doors and windows were actually created in the rock.

The sandstone privy at Holy Austin Rock.

Slots were cut into the sides to act as supports for the board seat over the bucket beneath. There is also a hole cut into the lowest part of the floor which, as the privy was prone to fill up with rainwater, allowed any flooding to run away down the hillside.

A climbing plant still grows over the entrance, not only providing a natural screen for the occupant from those in the dwellings, but also so that its welcome fragrance would hide the less pleasant bouquet emanating from the privy in the summer.

The site is tended by volunteers who do want to replace the board to make the privy more easily recognisable. Whilst there I chanced to meet with a local man whose family had been carpenters for a number of generations. He told me that his workshop used to contain a range of templates for cutting holes in privy boards. Apparently customers would try these holes for size, much the same as shoes are fitted today. Unfortunately these templates were among the first items to be disposed of when the gentleman retired.

A telephone call summoned me to Whiteladies Priory, near Brewood, where I was told the remnants of a garderobe could be found. And so it was I found myself driving to and fro along a narrow country lane in a vain attempt to locate these ruins. After several journeys along the road I happened to stop in order to study the map in greater detail when by pure chance I noticed a road sign lying in a ditch. As there was only one track off the road at this point I surmised that the elusive building must lie along here. So, locking my car, I followed the bridlepath. Once again I was on the point of giving up when the still imposing ruin loomed into view.

Whiteladies Priory was founded for Augustinian nuns around the beginning of the 12th century, the name referring to the colour of the undyed wool in which they dressed themselves.

The nunnery was dissolved in 1536 and afterwards the property was owned by a succession of Roman Catholic families. The house which replaced the priory was timber framed, and set in a walled garden. By the 18th century the house had been demolished and only the ruins of the small priory church remained, as they do to this day.

Whiteladies had its most important day, historically, in 1651 as it was the first hiding place of Charles II when he tried to flee the country following his defeat at the Battle of Worcester. He rested with the Penderel family for only a few hours until, suitably disguised, he was accompanied by Richard Penderel in an unsuccessful attempt to reach Wales.

If Charles had needed to answer a call of nature during his visit, it could not, however, have been at the garderobe still visible inset into the wall of the priory west of the main door. Originally this would have run off to a ditch or trench which was

Whiteladies Priory with the remains of the garderobe still visible on the right.

emptied periodically, or may even have been joined to a small watercourse. There are definite signs that such may well have been cut to take waste away from the priory, although without further archaeological evidence this remains unsure.

Mr Frederick Howell recalls lodgings in Victoria Road, Burton-on-Trent, where he lived for three years from 1927. Although every room had a water supply, there was no indoor toilet but a simple bucket privy at the end of the garden. For some reason unknown to Mr Howell, the landlady of the establishment insisted on the privy being locked whenever it was vacant (rather than the reverse as one would expect!). The key had to be obtained from her before anyone could 'go', and a strict rule enforced the return of the key to the owner immediately after-wards.

Mr Howell remembers the collecting vehicle as a two-wheeled cart drawn by one horse with two men in attendance. Viewed from the rear the collection receptacle on the cart was shaped like a flat-topped rounded bowl, although from above it would have appeared rectangular. As the base was rounded it rested on the sides of the cart, otherwise the container (and its contents) would have rocked to and fro (with doubtless spillages) as the cart moved along the cobbled street.

Owing to the awful smell from the cart, collection was always made at night. Whenever Mr Howell returned to Burton-on-Trent on a late train and, on entering Victoria Road, found a collection in progress, he always made an extended detour to reach his lodgings to allow time for the cart to move on.

[8]

YOU'RE TOO LATE

A visit to the village of Stanton, nestled away amongst the Staffordshire Moorlands, mirrored the typical scenario encountered whilst researching: 'There used to be one at . . .'; 'We've got one but it's now a . . .'.

Stanton, has, however, at least one privy still in use. Indeed this has been used by one person nearly all her adult life – over seventy years! Perhaps, therefore, it came as no surprise when she declined to comment. After such a period my request must have seemed an invasion on her privacy.

Nearby stood another brick privy, unfortunately no longer used. But, from the outside at least, one could see where access was gained by the night-soil man when emptying. Furthermore, the honeysuckle growing around the walls was the same plant which graced the small building when it was still in use. Fragrant plants were a feature of privies everywhere as a natural air freshener. In recent years the honeysuckle has been pruned back to a manageable level, but at one time would have discreetly hidden the little privy.

The Gilbert Sheldon School, now the village hall, has a small playground at the rear of which still stand both boys' and girls' toilets. Although in later years they were modernised to include both flush lavatories and wash basins, and are now in a state of disrepair, both clearly show they were originally earth closets. Supports for the boards (both one-holers, a pointer to the very small numbers who were educated here at any one time) are visible, as are the access holes for emptying. Sadly, once again too late.

Disused privy at a listed building in Uttoxeter. Nothing inside, only an inexplicable curtain!

The author's daughter, Sarah, at a privy in the Staffordshire Moorlands. Far from derelict, this privy is still in use and has recently had the near wall and roof slates repaired.

The former Gilbert Sheldon School toilets at Stanton, girls and boys entering the segregated building at different ends. The supports for the board seats are still visible.

Sometimes the details given stretched my detective talents to the limit in my attempts to trace an example. The journey to Bradnop to find Lower Ladies Meadow Farm seemed destined to end in disappointment, until a chance meeting with the local postman revealed this to be the only farm hereabouts which did not have its name along the roadside.

Having located the correct turning my hopes dropped once more when I found builders had almost completed their renovation. Another 'too late' seemed to be upon me until they pointed out the sturdy little construction of local stone away from the main house to the rear. After photographing what remained, including a small recess designed to hold a candle, I was turning to leave when an obviously old and quite hefty piece of wood

The farmhouse at Lower Ladies Meadow Farm was in the final stages of refurbishment. However, the privy had been cleaned out and the brickwork pointed. This two-holer also had a space in one wall where a candle provided meagre illumination on dark winter evenings.

caught my attention sticking out from a spoil heap. Borrowing a spade I managed to uncover enough of it to show it to be the missing board. Furthermore, when I eventually freed it I found it to be a two-holer.

On one occasion I was 'too late' for a particular privy building, which had been demolished, only to find that the board had been saved. What is more it now resides in the most unusual place.

At Waterfall I met a gentleman who pointed me in the direction of Cauldon and the Yew Tree Inn. I visited the establishment and on entering was astonished by the collection of memorabilia which met my eyes.

From the outside the Yew Tree is an unspectacular turn of the century establishment, somewhat overshadowed by the splendid yew in front of the building from which it takes its name. However, inside it is a virtual Aladdin's cave of pieces from a bygone era. Three distinct areas for customers are present, of which one is full of items collected by the owner from yesteryear. Old bicycles (including a penny-farthing), a mangle, washboard, nickleodeon, old slot machines, pictures, railway trinkets and even an old coal fire kitchen range take the attention from the more usual wall-mounted horse brasses.

Tucked away alongside the kitchen range, and almost directly beneath the dart board, I found the privy board. A two-holer in almost perfect condition. Apparently it came from a privy at Waterhouses belonging to a Doctor Bruce Richardson. When the doctor retired and moved away, his son modernised the toilet and was about to dispose of the board when the landlord from the Yew Tree asked if he might add it to his collection.

A visit to the Yew Tree, where a friendly welcome awaits, is further enhanced by a virtual guided tour of what must be the only private museum collection found within a pub.

A two-hole seat from Waterhouses, now under the dart board at the Yew Tree Inn and part of a wonderful collection of items from yesteryear within the pub.

Eunice Legerton's old privy at Burton upon Trent. Note the ventilation opening in the wall to the left of the door.

I visited another 'Yew Tree'; this time a small Victorian cottage, where a delightful brick-built privy still stands. The Staffordshire Federation of Women's Institutes had kindly printed an appeal for me in their County Newsletter, asking if any members had privies I could photograph. Several members generously responded; amongst them was Mrs Eunice Legerton who has not one but two privies in her back garden! Although the seat and bucket have long gone from the original privy, the exterior is lovingly preserved, together with other outbuildings including the 'modern' privy that still houses a bucket, but is now connected to a septic tank!

Mrs. Florence Hatchett, a member of Lichfield Women's Institute, has a privy in her garden which dates back to the 1870s. Honeysuckle planted outside the privy by her late husband soon after they moved to the property in 1940, flourishes on the outside walls. Intriguingly, the door to the privy carries the number 46.

BBC Radio Stoke has a wonderful weekday afternoon programme with a difference, presented by Barbara Adams. Much of the show is devoted to exploring the history of the area, with interviews and visits to fascinating places, revealing little known stories. I had the good fortune to meet Barbara, a truly delightfully effervescent lady, and she recalled one of her many visits to places of interest.

It was near Biddulph that Barbara visited a restored and renovated property which had once been the home of a character known to all and sundry as Fat Hannah. Her description may have become somewhat embroidered over the years but this

Mrs Florence Hatchett of Lichfield, standing beside her honeysuckle-covered privy.

woman was positively huge (one suggestion was 33 stones at the age of 22!).

When the new owners purchased the property it was in a very poor state. Consequently the first task was to clear out the accumulation of dust and rubbish. Amongst this they found a board from the privy. This had two or three holes of varying sizes to suit users of differing ages and genders. However, there was also one enormous hole which, I was assured, was large enough to pass over the man and his wife standing back-to-back without touching.

Sadly this was all that remained of the privy and that too has now been destroyed. Thus we shall never know what was under the board, unfortunate for it leaves me pondering as to how, with such a large hole, accuracy was ever assured. This may not have been a problem if there had been a simple pit. However, a bucket would have been another story.

At Upper Tean, near Cheadle, there once stood two octagonal privies, and this is probably my biggest disappointment in the 'too late' category. Facing each other on either side of the road, these privies had four compartments each (although some vaguely recalled there having been eight in earlier times, hence their shape). Each was served by a single collection pit, which was emptied 'whenever they had to'. Just why two such substantial public privies existed in what seems still to be a rather small place is a mystery. Some suggested one for each sex, but I got the impression this was more by deduction than fact. Sadly both of these buildings were demolished in the late 1980s.

To end this chapter, I am including the following letter I received from Anne Fisher, of Stone. Her privy unfortunately no longer exists but, as she says, memories linger on. There are undoubtedly many, many men and women, still healthily with us, who will share her view that, despite occasional horrors, the visit to the privy is still the most enduring and fondly recalled of childhood memories:

'The strange thing is that when I recall my childhood in a sixteenth-century farmhouse the room that comes most often to mind is the little brick privy that was fifty yards from the back door.

It was built of original hand-made bricks with a delapidated tile roof. Measuring about five foot by four it boasted an ill fitting wooden door with corners rounded away by age. The gaps so made were important because, when the door was shut, they provided the only source of light.

The scrubbed wooden seat had a large round hole that had originally suspended the user over an open trough. This trough was emptied infrequently and the contents spread on the fields with the cattle manure. In the mid Thirties we were modernised. The trough was filled in and a large, purpose built zinc bucket was strategically placed beneath the hole. This bucket was emptied each week and its emptying was the least popular job on the farm.

The whole structure was shrouded from prying eyes by a snowberry bush that waved eerily in the breeze, making frightening shadows on moonlit nights. Toilet paper was not for us. The *Farmers Weekly* was provided and to ensure that a good read could be had, it was not torn into small sheets but left in its entirety and placed temptingly to the side of the seat. My early reading experiences involved deciphering cattle adverts and studying fat stock prices!

What probably made our privy unique was the fact that the main railway line from London to Glasgow had been built less than ten yards from it. Wondering how the tenants of the 1840s had dared to use the privy when the line was first opened often stimulated my imagination. Though members of the family were quite used to sitting in state while the *Royal Scot* roared past rattling the tiles and rocking the building from side to side, it was quite another matter for visiting guests. Already convinced that the structure was unsafe, the effect of a passing goods train must have relieved many mild cases of constipation.

The thing that I have come to recognise as being of lasting value to me was the experience of making the last visit to the privy prior to going to bed. Leaving the warmth of the hearth to go out on a dark winter's night a whole new world would be revealed. The night sky, not masked by street lights, shone and twinkled above me. The noises of the night were there. The owls calling, little animals scurrying through the rough grass, cattle crunching hay in the barn. voices could be heard across the valley and the lamp-lit village houses looked warm and friendly. Many a time I would stand enthralled by the sense of peace and oneness with nature.

Other times, if I chose the right moment, I would hear a train steaming up the incline from Stafford and then see the light of its fires reflected in the billowing steam. The train would flash past giving me a chance to see passengers sitting talking, reading or, in the case of some lucky ones, eating in the buffet car. As a country child I could only guess at the journey these people were making and let my mind wander over bewitching possibilities.

Of course it was unhygienic and smelly but I know that little privy was very much a part of my childhood. I will never forget it and realise that my experences of it were yet another joy that the modern child will never know.'

[9]

SOME FINAL THOUGHTS

Throughout the ages much has been written about the right and wrong way of answering a call of nature. In fact it is only since Victorian times that such has been frowned upon as not for open discussion. Consider medieval times, for example, when public conveniences were anything but conveniently placed, and private loos lacked privacy.

During the times when only the rich and members of the church could in any respect be described as literate, it seems that hardly a borough in the land failed to cover the subject of toilet use in their statute books. Furthermore, with the ever-increasing population, efficient removal and disposal of the waste became of paramount importance, especially with a growing awareness of the health problem it was causing.

It seems odd that so much should be written at a time when very few other than the author could benefit from these words of wisdom, and the subject should become 'taboo' as more and more could benefit from the advice. A 15th-century volume dealing principally with matters of etiquette also touches on the subject of the toilet. The reader is warned of 'Draughty privys and of pyssynng in draughts,' which I presume was intended as an indication of the chill factor and not the proverbial 'getting one's own back'. The same source also gives the very sound advice to 'permyt no common pyssyng place about the house'. Amazing as it may seem today, even Elizabethan homes, rich as well as poor, still often had an area, usually the least used corner, where urination regularly took place. I wonder why it did not dawn on someone to place a bucket in the general vicinity. In the Tudor court a rule forbade any servant from

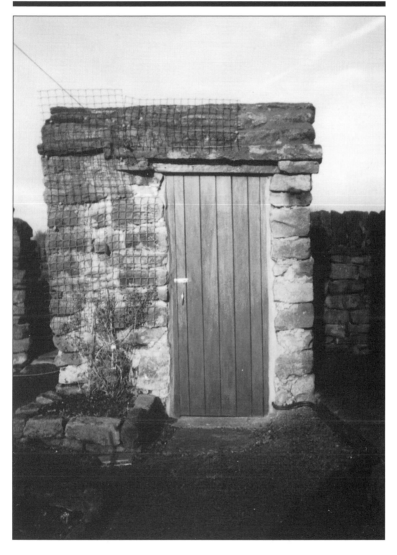

Lovingly restored as a tool shed, this former privy is 'in a vastly superior condition to when it was in constant use as a privy'.

'making water within the courts upon pain of one penny.' This was certainly a big step on the road to cleanliness.

The medieval period is noted for its lack of real medical knowledge. However, in their defence, it should be said they certainly made the best of what they had to hand. Virtually anyone with a trade dabbled in medicine, barbers it seems being particularly suited to double as physicians whenever the opportunity presented itself. When attempting to diagnose an illness their prognosis was invariably closely based on examining a urine sample. Calls of 'fill this' have therefore been sung for centuries, maybe more.

Urine has not always been regarded as merely a waste product. During the Middle Ages it was recycled as an early morning mouthwash by some. Yet a much earlier mention of urine collection and exploitation is found during the reign of the Roman emperor Vespasian (AD 69–79) who introduced the first known pay toilet at the Colosseum in Rome. This great amphitheatre not only profited by charging for relieving oneself but also received further financial gain by collecting the urine and selling it on to cloth-makers who used the liquid to remove the natural greasiness from the wool. One English school also records it collected the urine of the boys in the 17th century and sold it to tanners and dyers. The note firmly assures us all profits went into the school funds.

To be 'regular' may be good for the body, but apparently it does little for the soul. Saint Catherine of Sienna is reported to have visited the toilet as little as possible. It seems this was a penance she inflicted on herself in order to atone for all the wrongs she had done in her life. Clearly it did not prevent her from being canonised after her death.

The potty, or pysse potte as it was originally known, has proven an effective medium for comments by its designers. Whilst many potties have been preserved with an outstanding decorative design, presumably to distract from the contents, others also convey messages. Possibly the breakthrough for a previously unexplored area of humour, which has evolved into the virtual art form of toilet graffiti of the modern age.

One early 19th-century potty has in its inside base a portrait of a character with hands raised in shock, saying 'Oh dear me, what do I see?' From around the same time comes another literary gem: 'Keep me clean and use me well, And what I see I will not tell.'

In conversation one luncheon over a drink a gentleman told me a tale related to him by an elderly relative during his formative years. During Victorian times, he said, the urinals had a small design on them, a picture of a bee. Gentlemen were to aim in the direction of the bee in order to minimise the chance of splashing. Apparently I was not the first person to enquire 'Why a bee?' Indeed I began to doubt the sincerity of the account when told that the Latin for 'a bee' was – apis.

While travelling the county, I occasioned to visit a public toilet virtually decorated throughout with messages from previous patrons. One example which caught the eye was:

> Some come here to sit and think.
> Some come here to shit and stink.
> Some come here to scratch their balls.
> I come here to write on walls.

The above example shone out from a collection of initials, dates and ridiculous caricatures. Sadly the writing on the walls of public toilets is, to my mind, less imaginative than I remember from my youth. If only I could recall some actual examples from my school days ... Although, on reflection, adding them to this book would probably mean that I would be inundated with claims to copyright from the authors!

AND FINALLY ... I have come across a number of modern innovations which can all be seen as simple updates of the humble privy. One of the most common is the decorative toilet. Here bold and starkly contrasting colours are used in an abstract style, with the result that the toilet itself is either highlighted or camouflaged.

However, the prize for the most novel idea must go to Screwy-loos, who produce a range of toilet seats but with an important difference. The normal coloured-plastic or wooden styles have been replaced by a transparent or opaque seat, within which an almost endless array of items are positioned. Virtually anything is possible, provided it is small enough to be enclosed by the seat. Leaves, flowers and grasses are popular subjects, while shells, nuts and bolts, kitchen cutlery, artificial jewellery and newspaper cuttings have all been tried successfully. My particular favourite features a coil of barbed wire in a transparent seat – which certainly makes the first-time user think twice before sitting.

A Privy By Any Other Name

A 'certain' place
Asterroom
Aunt Jane's
Biffy Bog
Boghouse
Bombay
Chamberlain pianos ('bucket
  lav')
Chamber of commerce
Chuggie
Closet
Cludgie
Comfort station
Crapphouse
Crapping castle
Dike
Dinkum-dunnies
Doneks
Dover House
Dubby
Dubs
Duffs
Dunnakin
Dunnekin

Dunnick
Dyke
Garden loo
Garderobe
Go and have a Jimmy Riddle
Go and have a Tom Tit
Going to pick daisies
Going to see a man about a
  dog
Going to stack the tools
Going to the George
Going to the groves
Gone where the wind is always
  blowing
Gong
Gong house
Heads
Here is are
Holy of holies
Home of rest
Honk
House of commons
House of office
Houses of parliament

Jakes
Jericho
Jerry-come-tumble
Karzi
Klondike
Knickies
Larties
Latrine
Lav
Lavatory
Little house
Loo
My aunts
Nessy
Netty
Out the back
Petty
Place of easement
Place of repose
Place of retirement
Reading room
Round-the-back
Shit-hole
Shittush
Shooting gallery
Shunkie
Slash house
The backhouse

The boggy at the bottom
The bush
The dispensary
The dunny
The grot
The halting station Hoojy-boo
    (attributed to Dame Edith
    Evans)
The house where the emperor
    goes on foot
The hum
The jakers
The jampot
The japping
The John
The lats
The long drop
The opportunity
The ping-pong house
The proverbial
The Sammy
The shants
The shot-tower
The sociable
The tandem (a two-holer)
The thinking house
The throne room
The watteries

The wee house
The whajucallit
Three and more seaters
Thunder box
Tivvy
Two seaters
Widdlehouse
Windsor Castle
'Yer Tiz'

The penny house
The plumbing
The porcelain pony
The urinal
The water box
Umtag (Russian version of the WC)
Waterloo

Especially for WCs:
Adam & Eve
Chain of events
Flushes and blushes
Going to inspect the plumbing

The term 'privy' is an Early Middle English word which derives from the Latin 'privatus' meaning apart or secret.

ACKNOWLEDGEMENTS

Thanks are due to Nicholas Battle, without whose suggestion this book would never have been written, and to my daughter Sarah, without whom my travels would have been very lonely. Acknowledgements are also due to all those who have contributed, with special mentions for Barbara Adams of BBC Radio Stoke; to Bob Meason for innumerable leads; and to Terence Thompson who virtually covered Burton-on-Trent for me.

Finally, special thanks go to Staffordshire Federation of Women's Institutes for their assistance and to those W.I. members who contacted me with privy memories and with photographs.